Dreaming of
HORSES

NICOLA JANE SWINNEY

PHOTOGRAPHY BY BOB LANGRISH

FIREFLY BOOKS

A FIREFLY BOOK

Published by Firefly Books Ltd., 2019

Text © Nicola Jane Swinney

Copyright © Marshall Editions 2015

First printing

Library of Congress Control Number: 2019938801

Library and Archives Canada Cataloguing in Publication

Title: Dreaming of horses / Nicola Jane Swinney ; photography by Bob Langrish.

Names: Swinney, Nicola Jane, author. | Langrish, Bob, photographer.

Description: Includes index.

Identifiers: Canadiana 20190098686 | ISBN 9780228102090 (softcover)

Subjects: LCSH: Horses—Juvenile literature. | LCSH: Horse breeds—Juvenile literature.

Classification: LCC SF291 .S93 2019 | DDC j636.1—dc23

Published in Canada by
Firefly Books Ltd.
50 Staples Avenue, Unit 1
Richmond Hill, Ontario
L4B 0A7

Published in the United States by
Firefly Books (U.S.) Inc.
P.O. Box 1338, Ellicott Station
Buffalo, New York
14205

Printed in China

CONTENTS

ᴬ HORSE BY OUR SIDE

Without the horse, the world we live in today would be very different. Since humans first realized that these animals would make an ideal form of transportation, equines have been our constant companions. They have been by our side—or, rather, underneath us—in war, in adventure, in sports, and in leisure throughout our history.

SHAPED BY PLACES AND PEOPLE

The climate and terrain have shaped the breeds of each country, from the Arabian of the desert, which has contributed so much to the world's equines, to England's hardy little Exmoor pony.

But we have shaped the horse for our own needs, too. The heavy horses needed to carry armored warriors into battle have been replaced by the sleek Thoroughbred for racing and the athletic warmblood for competition. We require the beauty of the black Friesian to add pomp to ceremonial carriages, or the dancing white Lipizzaner for our entertainment.

IN PRAISE OF THE HORSE

We are lucky that such creatures, whose size and strength could easily overcome us, are happy to work with us and for us. Perhaps the author and poet Ronald Duncan put it best, when he wrote his poem *In Praise of the Horse* in 1954: "Where in this wide world can man find nobility without pride, friendship without envy, or beauty without vanity? Here, where grace is laced with muscle and strength by gentleness confined…"

Founding
Breeds

Most modern breeds of horses are based on the Arabian. This includes the mighty Thoroughbred, which in turn has influenced other breeds and is still used to refine more common stock.

THE ARABIAN

The Arabian is believed to be the oldest breed of horse in the world today. It was bred to be a desert horse and can live on little food. Because it lived close to the Bedouin—traveling desert people—it developed a bond with humans. It dates back more than 5,000 years and has influenced many modern breeds.

A CLEVER HORSE

Arabian horses are intelligent and learn quickly, so they are easy to train, but they are fiery and highly strung, too. They bond with their owner or trainer and tend to be loyal and affectionate. Although Arabians are not always suitable for someone just starting to ride, since they can be a little "sharp," they do make great competition horses.

TRADITIONAL TACK

To the Bedouin, the Arabian horse was prized above rubies. The breeders of these glorious creatures were proud of them and showed them off in colorful tack, decorated with rosettes, beads, shells, and tassels.

THE MOVEMENT

The Arabian horse's action is so smooth that it is said to float. It also has another desirable trait called "elevation"—its trot is high off the ground. As well as being elegant in its movement, the breed is known for its speed and stamina.

THE HEAD

The Arabian's head is easily recognizable. It has large, beautiful eyes—often called "liquid" eyes—small, neat ears, and wide nostrils. The shield-shaped bulge on its forehead is unique to Arabians and is called the *jibbah*. It is a very desirable feature that Arabian breeders and owners look out for.

THE AKHAL-TEKE

Some people believe this glorious breed is even older than the Arabian. The bones of these tall, finely boned horses were found in southern Turkmenistan in central Asia, dating from 2,400 B.C. With its clean, spare lines and shimmering coat, it rivals the Arabian for beauty and grace.

THE LEGEND

This unusual breed has always attracted headlines. When one called Melekush was given as a gift to Queen Elizabeth II of the United Kingdom in 1956, her grooms thought that the horse's beautiful gleaming coat had been treated with some kind of polish. They gave it a bath—which made its coat shine all the more.

THE NAME

The word "Akhal" comes from a long oasis that was found in the foothills of the Kopet Dag Mountains, once part of Persia. "Teke" is after the nomadic Turkmen people who lived in the oasis and bred and raised their unique horses. Turkmenistan is fairly isolated, with the Caspian Sea to the west, mountains to the south, and desert to the north. This means that the breed has remained largely free of outside influence.

FACT FILE

HEIGHT: up to 16hh

COLOR: most commonly a golden dun or chestnut, but other solid colors too

CHARACTER: fiery, intelligent, loyal

USES: endurance, racing, riding, showing

THE FAME

The Akhal-Teke was prized by rulers throughout history. Alexander the Great's magnificent horse Bucephalus is thought to have been an Akhal-Teke, and the breed was also used by Genghis Khan, Marco Polo, Roman emperors, and many others. Some historians believe the Byerley Turk, one of the founders of the Thoroughbred breed, was actually an Akhal-Teke.

THE THOROUGHBRED

Horse racing is one of the biggest equine "industries" in the world. People gamble huge amounts of money on the outcome of a contest between some of the most beautiful creatures ever to walk the earth. Many of these ultimate athletes are Thoroughbreds—a breed that is the result of four centuries of selective breeding.

THE LINEAGE

Almost all modern Thoroughbreds can trace their lineage back to just three stallions: the Byerley Turk, the Darley Arabian, and the Godolphin Arabian. These horses were named after the men who owned them. The Byerley Turk (which was probably actually an Arabian) was ridden into battle by Captain Byerley in 1690. The Darley Arabian was bought by Thomas Darley in Aleppo (now Syria) in 1704. The Godolphin Arabian was purchased by Lord Godolphin. In 1850, it was said that "the blood of the Godolphin Arabian is in every stable in England."

FACT FILE

HEIGHT: around 16hh

COLOR: all solid colors except palomino

CHARACTER: intelligent, spirited, trainable

USES: racing, eventing, hunting

THE AMERICAN FOUNDATION

The first Thoroughbred to reach North America was Bulle Rock, a son of the Darley Arabian. He was brought to Virginia by Samuel Gist in 1730. Bulle Rock was 21 years old at the time, but he had been a successful racehorse in his youth in Britain. By 1800, a further 338 Thoroughbreds had been imported.

AN EQUINE POWERHOUSE

The Thoroughbred is a supreme athlete that can gallop at almost 40 mi. (64 km) per hour, a speed it can maintain for distances of 1 mi. (1.6 km) or more. The original Arabian blood gave it speed and stamina, as well as its undeniable beauty. Those early influences can be seen in its intelligent eyes, and in the clean, hard limbs and good feet.

THE ANDALUSIAN

The Andalusian is a magnificent athlete: a perfect, living machine and the very picture of equine beauty. The seamless bond early warriors had with this breed of horse is thought to be where the myth of the centaur—half man, half horse—came from. The Andalusian is such a good-looking horse that it is little wonder it is known as the aristocrat of the equine world.

THE HISTORY

There were horses on the Iberian Peninsula—Spain and Portugal—as far back as 25,000 B.C. The Andalusian was prized as a cavalry horse and was the chosen horse of European rulers. But the breed nearly died out because of cross-breeding and being used so much in the Napoleonic wars. Luckily, it was saved by a group of monks, who ensured the good bloodlines were not lost.

THE BODY

The Andalusian has long, sloping shoulders with prominent withers, rounded hindquarters, and strong legs with short cannon bones. All these features combine to make it a superb equine athlete.

FACT FILE

HEIGHT: 15hh to 16.2hh

COLOR: gray, black, bay, chestnut

CHARACTER: intelligent, calm

USES: cavalry, dressage, parade, bullfighting

THE MOVEMENT

The Andalusian has a dazzling, high-stepping action and can really cover the ground. It is seen at its beautiful best in the fiestas—or festivals—in its Spanish homeland, but it also excels in the show ring and the dressage arena. It has been used for centuries in the bullring, where its athletic ability keeps it at a safe distance from the bull.

THE HEAD

Noble and elegant, the Andalusian's beautiful head is balanced and refined without being dainty. It has none of the convex appearance of its Portuguese cousin, the Lusitano. It is set on an arched and powerful neck.

Wild ————— and Feral Horses

Sadly, there are no longer any truly "wild" horses. Humans have been so successful in domesticating the horse that even those that roam free are feral: the descendants of once tame horses that have returned to their natural, wild state.

THE MUSTANG

The Mustang is the unofficial national horse of the United States, having roamed free across the country for centuries. The name "Mustang" comes from the Spanish word *mesteño*, meaning "wild" or "stray," because it is descended from stray horses that were originally brought to the Americas in the 1500s by Spanish explorers.

THE MELTING POT

Over the last 400 years, many other breeds have added to the melting pot that makes up the Mustang. The original Spanish horses were probably a mix of Andalusian, Lusitano, Alter-Real, and Sorraia. But French settlers also brought horses with them and the United States government bought heavy German horses to pull heavy artillery, both of which have mixed with the breed.

THE COLOR

Many different colors appear in the modern Mustang, including piebald and skewbald. Even today, the occasional gray-dun or grullo can be seen—a color that echoes that of the original Sorraia horse breed.

FACT FILE

HEIGHT: 14hh

COLOR: all colors

CHARACTER: hardy, lively, intelligent

USES: wild horse

THE THREAT

Wonderful as they are to see, in the past, the Mustangs were thought of as pests. In the early 1900s, food was scarce and cattle had to share the plains with around two million wild horses. This meant the ranchers started shooting the horses, to leave more grazing room for their cattle. Fortunately, today the Mustang is protected by law.

THE HEAD

The little horse usually has a dainty head, almost pony-like, but the influence of so many breeds on the Mustang means that there are many differences between horses.

THE CHINCOTEAGUE

Marguerite Henry's delightful novel *Misty of Chincoteague* ensured that this little creature, who actually lives on Assateague Island, off the coast of Virginia, has a lasting place in our hearts. But no one really knows how the ponies came to be on the island in the first place.

THE LEGEND

It is widely believed that the ponies came to the island from a wrecked ship. A Spanish galleon called *La Galga* sank off the coast of Virginia in 1750 and, shortly afterwards, ponies appeared on the beaches of Assateague. The wreck of *La Galga* is thought to be buried on the island.

THE CHILD'S PONY

Although the Chincoteague is a feral horse that roams wild on the island, it is gentle and calm and makes an ideal child's pony. It usually stands around 12 to 13 hands tall, so it is a very good choice for smaller riders. It is also used to surviving on not much food, so isn't as expensive to keep as some breeds.

ISLAND LIFE

The ponies live on the island of Assateague, which is shared between the states of Maryland and Virginia. There are two herds—one lives at the Maryland end, and the other at the Virginia end. Each summer, the Virginia herd is swum across a channel to the nearby Chincoteague Island by "saltwater cowboys," to the cheers and applause of thousands of spectators.

THE FUTURE

Once the ponies reach Chincoteague, the foals are auctioned off. There are around 70 foals born every year and three-quarters of them will be sold. Some will be "buybacks"—the new owner agrees to give the pony back to the herd to keep the bloodlines healthy. The buyback foals are often the most expensive.

FACT FILE

HEIGHT: 12hh to 13hh

COLOR: all colors

CHARACTER: gentle, robust, easy keepers

USES: riding, harness

THE BRUMBY

There are various stories that explain how the iconic wild horse of Australia got its name. There were no horses on this vast continent until the "First Fleet" of ships from Great Britain landed in 1788. These ships contained criminals who had been deported, along with various livestock and supplies. The early horses were of Thoroughbred blood and only the toughest survived the long, hard voyage.

THE MYTH BEHIND THE NAME

Their alien new world was huge and largely barren. The few fences that were there proved inadequate and many horses escaped, becoming feral. A British soldier called James Brumby, who was also a farrier, owned several horses. He moved from New South Wales to Tasmania in the 1800s, leaving some horses behind. When people asked who these horses belonged to, they were told "they're Brumby's." The name may also have derived from "baroomby," the Aboriginal word for "wild."

FACT FILE

HEIGHT: all heights

COLOR: all colors

CHARACTER: feral

USES: feral, though some have been successfully rehomed and trained

MOBS OR BANDS

Brumby horses became plentiful in Australia. They were fast, hardy, and resourceful, evading capture. Because they were inbred, they kept their wild tendencies and proved difficult to tame, making them unsuitable as riding horses. They traveled in large groups—known as mobs or bands—each of which had a senior stallion, mares, and young colts. In time, these colts would fight the stallion for control of the band.

HARSH REALITIES

Unfortunately, the wild Brumby was considered a pest, and still is by many people. They compete with livestock for meager food supplies and precious water. Their hard hooves wear paths through the outback, where they are not wanted, and they can spread disease. Numbers are controlled by the Australian government. There are thought to be at least 600,000 wild Brumbies in Australia today.

THE CAMARGUE

They look like pale ghosts as they move through the mist at the delta of the Rhone River in southern France. These are the Camargue horses, named for the triangle of water and marsh where the Rhone meets the Mediterranean. They are known as "the Horses of the Sea," and the breed is one of the oldest in the world. Equines have existed in this harsh and unforgiving region since prehistoric times, and the Camargue is thought to have descended from the now-extinct Solutré Horse, about which little is known.

ANCIENT HISTORY

Throughout history, many armies have passed through this region, including the Greeks, Romans, and Arabs. The horses they brought with them undoubtedly had some influence on the Camargue, although there is little evidence of Arabian blood. But they have remained remarkably uniform. It has also been suggested that the Camargue has influenced the horses of Spain, since the invading armies took some of them home when they returned.

FACT FILE

HEIGHT: 14hh

COLOR: always gray

CHARACTER: tough, intelligent, kind

USES: riding, herding

WHITE HORSES

Camargue horses run wild in small herds across the marshes, which are either scorched by the sun or lashed with icy winds blowing off the Alps. The herds are formed of a stallion, his mares, and their offspring. Foals are born from April to July and are dark brown or black. Their coat lightens with age, until they become almost pure white in maturity. They are small animals, shaped by their harsh environment, but tough and hardy.

PROTECTED BREED

In 1928, the wetlands where the Camargue horses roam were declared a national park, and the horses and the area's fierce little black bulls became protected species. Today, the foals are branded at one year old and at three are corralled and trained. Colts or stallions judged not suitable for breeding are gelded. The Camargue breed is still protected today.

THE EXMOOR

Some 100,000 years ago, horses arrived in what is now England. They arrived by crossing the swampy land that later became the English Channel, long before the country was cut off from the rest of Europe. Those first equines are thought to have changed very little. Archaeological evidence dating back over 60,000 years reveals horses that bear an uncanny resemblance to the Exmoor pony of today.

ISOLATED ISLANDS

The world changed a great deal through the millennia, with various invading armies and their horses influencing British breeds. In the past few centuries, the trade routes that crossed the United Kingdom brought foreign equine blood, too. But on inhospitable Exmoor, in the West Country of England, the wild ponies were largely free from outside influence. No new breeds were introduced to refine or improve existing stock.

BUILT TO LAST

There are few creatures designed to survive harsh conditions better than the Exmoor pony. Its eyes are hooded—sometimes called "toad eyes"—to protect them from snow and wind. It grows a thick, double-layered coat in the winter to keep it warm and dry, and its tail has a snow-chute (also called an ice-tail)—a group of short, coarse hairs at the top, designed to draw snow and ice away from its body. This, and the double-layered coat, are shed in the summer, to be regrown in the autumn.

A RARE BREED

The Exmoor has had mixed fortunes during its long history and today is considered "critical" by the Rare Breeds Survival Trust. During World War II, the wild ponies on the moor were used as target practice by the British military trainees. By the end of the war, only around 50 remained. The ponies today still live free on the moor, but they are carefully monitored by the Exmoor Pony Society and part of Exmoor is now a national park.

FACT FILE

HEIGHT: up to 12.3hh

COLOR: brown with mealy (oatmeal) muzzle and black points

CHARACTER: alert, intelligent, kind

USES: the Exmoor makes an excellent child's pony, but can carry an adult, too

THE NEW FOREST

Ponies have roamed the forests of southern England since the end of the last Ice Age, roughly 10,000 years ago. These are known as the New Forest ponies, or simply "Foresters," and without them the New Forest itself would be very different—more overgrown, with fewer birds and flowers. The ponies' and the forest's fortunes are intertwined.

ANCIENT HISTORY

Bones of a pony standing around 13hh were found at a Roman villa in Rockbourne, Hampshire. Centuries later, the profits of the Royal Stud at Lyndhurst went toward building Beaulieu Abbey, founded in 1204. The earliest record of ponies in the New Forest is from 1016, when the rights of common pasture allowed local people to graze their animals in the forest.

FACT FILE

HEIGHT: up to 14.2hh

COLOR: bay, brown, gray, chestnut, roan, black

CHARACTER: intelligent, willing, gentle

USES: they make excellent first ponies for children, gymkhana, driving, show jumping, dressage

FAMOUS BLOODLINES

Over the centuries, as with many British breeds, different stallions have been introduced to "improve" the ponies. Among the most notable is Marske—sire of the great racehorse Eclipse—who was sold to a farmer in Ringwood, Hampshire, when his owner, the Duke of Cumberland, died. Marske was used on "country mares" until his most famous son started winning.

UNCERTAIN FUTURE

There are thought to be fewer than 3,000 breeding adult ponies, making the New Forest's future look uncertain. They still roam free in the forest, but are owned privately by the local Commoners. Each autumn, the ponies are rounded up in a process called the Drift, so that they can be checked over for general health and treated if necessary.

America's
Horses

There were no horses at all in the Americas until the late 15th century, but the range of breeds now found there is truly impressive. American breeders have produced some of the most glorious equines in the world.

THE MORGAN

In the past, there was a fashion for animals to be referred to by their owner's name. The legendary horse that was the start of a famous American breed was known as "the Justin Morgan horse," even though his real name was Figure. And "legend" is not too strong a word: this powerful, compact little creature was renowned far and wide. He was by a Thoroughbred stallion, with Welsh Cob and Friesian influences.

THE BEGINNING

Figure belonged to Justin Morgan of Vermont and is thought to have been foaled in 1789. His sire was a stallion called True Briton, also known as Beautiful Bay. True Briton was an English Thoroughbred, and was described by Morgan as "a curious horse." The resulting colt was to go on to found America's first horse breed.

FACT FILE

HEIGHT: up to 15.2hh

COLOR: all colors

CHARACTER: alert, intelligent, kind

USES: riding, showing, ranching, driving

THE LEGEND

Stories of "the Morgan horse's" strength, speed, and stamina quickly spread. His owner raced him and hired him out for logging and farm work. The horse stood barely 14hh, but he seemed tireless and could out-walk, out-trot, out-run, and out-pull almost every other horse. He also produced offspring that resembled him, both in looks and nature.

THE BREED

Figure's foals were highly sought-after and the "Morgan horses" became recognized as a breed. They were compact and hardy—Figure himself lived to the age of 32, despite a lifetime of hard work—but refined and elegant in appearance. They were known for their sweet temper and trainability.

THE QUARTER HORSE

One of the most iconic American breeds, the Quarter Horse gets its name from the distance of one-on-one races that were popular in the late 1600s. They were run along streets, country lanes, and on level pastures, and were no longer than a quarter of a mile. The fastest of these animals were known originally as Celebrated American Running Horses.

BIG BUSINESS

A great deal of money changed hands over these one-on-one races, with huge bets placed. Some of the grand plantations may have changed hands as a result of these contests! Disagreements and fights were not unheard of, although the quality of the horses was one thing everyone could agree on. As well as being fast, these compact horses were generally good-looking, too.

MOVING WEST

During the 1800s, huge cattle ranches were set up all over the Western Plains. The Quarter Horse, which had great stamina, also proved to have another desirable trait—what was known as "cow sense," the ability to out-maneuver cattle. The horse was agile and easy to train, and it soon became the mount of choice for ranchers.

THE MODERN BREED

With its combination of speed and strength, the Quarter Horse is described as a powerhouse with a "sanity button." Although spirited, the breed is renowned for being calm and accommodating, making it ideal for the beginner rider. It has become admired worldwide for these attributes and its versatility makes it suitable for work or pleasure.

FACT FILE

HEIGHT: 15.1hh

COLOR: most solid colors, with little white marking

CHARACTER: spirited, intelligent, loyal

USES: ranching, trail riding, showing, trekking

THE SADDLEBRED

This breed, which has its roots in the 1600s, was originally known simply as "the American Horse." It is based on the gaited horses known as Narragansett Pacers, which were founded in the Rhode Island area of the same name, crossed with Thoroughbreds. The new breed became more refined than the pacers, but retained their comfortable gait. High-stepping and elegant, the Saddlebred is the ultimate show horse.

THE VERSATILE BREED

Whether it is in the dressage arena, eventing, show jumping, endurance, or driving, the Saddlebred will do anything that is asked of it. But it is at showing that it excels—it got its nickname, "the peacock of the show ring," for a reason!

THE COMFORTABLE PACE

Like all of America's gaited breeds, the Saddlebred moves its legs at the same time on each side. This is different from the lateral trot, in which the front and hind legs move on the diagonal. It means that there is less jolting, which makes the gait supremely comfortable.

HISTORY ON HIS BACK

It was these "American Horses" that carried the Colonial cavalry to victory over the British in the Battle of King's Mountain in South Carolina in 1780. And in the Civil War, American generals rode Saddlebred horses, among them General Robert E. Lee's famous Traveller. After the war the soldiers took their horses home with them, to spread the breed across the United States.

FACT FILE

HEIGHT: 14hh to 17hh

COLOR: all colors

CHARACTER: intelligent, kind, alert

USES: dressage, eventing, carriage driving, show jumping, showing

THE TENNESSEE WALKING HORSE

There can be few more instantly recognizable American breeds than the Tennessee Walking Horse, sometimes known as simply "the Walker." It was the first horse breed to bear the name of an American state. It is one of the many "gaited" horses—those that possess another gait or gaits as well as the standard walk, trot, canter, and gallop.

THE BEGINNING

Various other breeds and types of horse came together to make the modern Tennessee Walker. Among them were the now-defunct Narragansett Pacer, Canadian Pacer, Morgan, Standardbred, and Saddlebred. The Walking Horse was popular with plantation owners, who would ride around their land inspecting crops, and needed a comfortable mode of transportation.

THE GAITS

It is said of the Tennessee Walking Horse that "if you ride one today, you will buy one tomorrow," because it is so comfortable. Its three exceptional gaits are the flat-foot walk, the running walk, and a smooth canter. It is the running walk for which it is most famous. Smooth and gliding, the horse can reach speeds of up to 20 mi. (32 km) per hour. All gaits are inherited, not taught.

GENTLE BEAUTY

The Tennessee Walker has an endearing, gentle nature, so it is ideal as a family horse or a mount for novice or nervous riders. The original animals were probably rather plain, since they were for use rather than show. But the modern Walker is a beautiful creature, with a refined, elegant head, intelligent eye, and graceful neck.

FACT FILE

HEIGHT: 14.3hh to 17hh

COLOR: all colors

CHARACTER: gentle, kind, easy

USES: riding, showing, Western riding, ranching

THE APPALOOSA

Native Americans can proudly claim credit for this iconic American breed, whose lavishly spotted coat is prized around the world. The Nez Perce were acknowledged as the only tribe to selectively breed their horses, and they wanted nothing but the best—the strongest, fastest, and most sure-footed.

COLORFUL HISTORY

The Nez Perce entered into a treaty with the U.S. government in 1855, which gave the tribe 7 million acres (2.8 million ha) of land. But in 1860, gold was discovered on the reservation, and with it came an influx of settlers, breaching the treaty. The tribe's lands were reduced, and battles broke out. The chief surrendered in 1877 and the tribe's horses were confiscated. The Nez Perce were banned from owning the spotted horses, a law that was not lifted until 1991.

DISTINCTIVE PATTERNS

Instantly identifiable by its spots, the Appaloosa must have three other characteristics: white sclera (around the eye), mottled skin, and striped hooves. There are seven recognized coat patterns: blanket, spots, blanket with spots, roan, roan blanket, roan blanket with spots, and solid, but there are also 13 base coat colors.

A PALOUSE HORSE

The name Appaloosa wasn't coined until the 1900s. The spotted horses were seen in great numbers around the Palouse River, which flowed through Eastern Washington and Northern Idaho. The white settlers referred to them as "a Palouse horse," which eventually became "apalousey horse," and the name Appaloosa was adopted. Claude Thompson, a wheat farmer from Oregon, established the Appaloosa Horse Club in 1938 to promote the breed.

FACT FILE

HEIGHT: 14hh and over

COLOR: 13 base colors, 7 coat patterns

CHARACTER: alert, clever, spirited

USES: riding, show jumping, trekking, ranching

THE PALOMINO

It is said that its coat shines like a newly minted 14-karat gold coin, and this color in horses is almost as old as the first equines. It has been depicted in artworks, featured in Greek mythology, coveted by ancient emperors, kings, and queens, treasured by ancient tribes, and brought to the Americas by the conquistadors. Elvis Presley, "The King" himself, owned a Palomino called Rising Sun.

THE HISTORY

Queen Isabella of Spain adored these golden horses and, even today, the color is sometimes called "Isabella." Back in the 15th century, she sold her jewels to fund the expedition of Christopher Columbus that led to the discovery of the Americas. But the breed is far older than that. When Richard the Lionheart, king of England in the 1100s, retook Jerusalem in 1192, it is said that the defeated Muslim leader Saladin gave him two horses—one a gray, the other a golden Palomino.

JUST FOR ROYALTY

The horses owned by Queen Isabella of Spain in the 15th century were known as "Golden Dorado," and she had 500 of them. She sent a stallion and five mares to her viceroy in New Spain (which is now Mexico) so the breed could prosper in the New World. She thought so highly of those beautiful creatures that she forbade non-royals—or commoners—to own one.

FACT FILE

HEIGHT: 14hh to 17hh

COLOR: variations of gold with white mane and tail

CHARACTER: depends on breeding

USES: all riding

THE COLOR

Many believe that Palomino is a coat color, but in the United States it is considered a breed, and its bloodlines are carefully protected. Although many breeds carry the Palomino gene, about 50 percent of registered Palominos are Quarter Horses. Palomino is based on a chestnut coat color: crossing a chestnut horse with a cremello (a pale cream) will sometimes produce a Palomino. The color varies from a pale shimmering gold to a deep, rich copper, set off by a white or ivory mane and tail.

THE PAINT

Herds of colored horses once roamed the Western Plains and deserts of North America, but were later domesticated. Native Americans revered striking, broken-coated horses, believing them to have magic powers. The Comanche tribe, considered by many authorities to be the finest riders of the American plains, possessed many of these creatures, and they are depicted on the painted buffalo robes the tribe used as historical records.

HERDING AND RANCHING

Descended from Spanish stock and introduced to the New World by the conquistadors, this tough little horse was prized by the cowboys for its strength and agility. Many of the colored horses that roamed so freely in the 1800s were of "stock" type: compact, short-coupled, and strong, with good bones and a sound constitution. They were athletic and willing and made excellent cow ponies, for herding and ranching cattle.

THE PATTERNS

There are two main types of coat pattern in the modern Paint horse: tobiano and overo. The tobiano horse has a solid-colored head, sometimes with a star or blaze, four white legs, strong markings, including dark flanks, and its tail is often two colors. The overo will not have white on its back between the withers and the tail, one or all four legs will be dark, its markings will be splashy and its face may be white. The terms "piebald" and "skewbald" originate from the word "bald" used to describe a white face.

FACT FILE

HEIGHT: all heights

COLOR: tobiano, overo, tovero (a mix of both)

CHARACTER: intelligent, kind, athletic

USES: pleasure riding, rodeo, trail, racing, showing

THE MODERN PAINT

The first official American Paint Horse was a black and white tobiano stallion called Bandits Pinto, owned by the Flying M Ranch of McKinney, Texas. It was recorded in 1962, when a society to protect and enhance the breed was started. The American Paint Horse Association wanted to ensure that the breed was not entirely based on coat patterns, so they set strict standards of conformation, athletic ability, temperament, and performance.

THE FALABELLA

Small but mighty, the Falabella is most definitely a horse, not a pony, despite its tiny frame. Like most of the American breeds, it originated from the Spanish horses brought to the New World in the 16th century, some of which were either released or escaped. The harsh conditions of the plains in Argentina, known as the pampas, made these horses into tough little creatures that could survive the unforgiving sun and the strong winds—El Pampero—that roared across the landscape.

TOUGH EXISTENCE

They were undoubtedly shaped by their harsh environment. The vast expanse of the pampas offered little in the way of food or water, so the herds had to travel huge distances. Those that faltered or fell did not make it. Those that were left—short in stature, stocky, and resilient—formed the basis of the modern Falabella. There may also have been genetic reasons for their size, caused by inbreeding among the herds.

FACT FILE

HEIGHT: up to 22 in. (56 cm)

COLOR: all colors

CHARACTER: sweet-natured, gentle, good with children

USES: pets, showing

TINY HORSES

In the 1840s, an Irish settler in Argentina, Patrick Newell, noticed the herds of small horses around the capital, Buenos Aires. He rounded up the smallest ones he could find and began a breeding program to produce level, consistent stock. He was a knowledgeable horseman and passed this knowledge, as well as his tiny horses, to his son-in-law, Juan Falabella, who in turn passed them on to his son, Emilio, then to his son, Julio. Over the years, the family improved and refined their little horses.

OUTSIDE INFLUENCE

Other equine blood was used during the centuries, including the tough Criollo (Argentina's national breed, also Spanish in origin), Appaloosa, and Welsh Mountain Pony. The breed was introduced to North America in the 1960s, where it found instant fame. The Falabella today is considered rare, with fewer than 1,500 registered with the breed society.

THE PONY OF THE AMERICAS

A foal called Black Hand founded America's favorite pony breed. A Shetland breeder from Iowa named Les Boomhower was offered an Arabian/Appaloosa mare who had been bred to a Shetland stallion. When the foal, a colt, was born, it was white with black splashes on its coat, one of which looked like a handprint. Les named it Black Hand.

HOW IT BEGAN

Boomhower contacted other Shetland breeders and they formed the Pony of the Americas Club in 1954. His vision was to produce a pony breed for children to ride and show—adults could only show the ponies in-hand or driven. To be suitable for children, the pony had to be gentle and easy to train.

FACT FILE

HEIGHT: up to 56 in. (142 cm)

COLOR: as with the Appaloosa

CHARACTER: kind, gentle, trainable

USES: showing, riding, driving

STRICT GUIDELINES

For an animal to be registered as a Pony of the Americas (POA), it had to be between 44 and 52 in. (118 to 132 cm) in height. Its head should be small and dished, like that of an Arabian, and its body muscled like that of a Quarter Horse. It must also have Appaloosa-like markings that are visible from a distance of 40 ft. (12 m).

ROARING SUCCESS

The POA proved a huge success from the start. It has grown in stature, as well as popularity: the maximum height has been increased to 56 in. (142 cm). Less Shetland blood is used in the modern POA, with more Welsh, Quarter Horse, and Appaloosa influence to achieve the look of a little horse rather than a pony. The POA Club motto is: "Try hard, win humbly, lose gracefully, and, if you must, protest with dignity." Which is not a bad motto for life itself!

THE PASO FINO

It is known as the "horse of the fine walk" and is one of the most celebrated gaited breeds of the Americas. On his second voyage from Spain in 1493, Christopher Columbus brought with him a select group of horses from Andalusia and Cordela in Spain, and settled them at Santo Domingo in the Dominican Republic. They were a mixture of Spanish breeds, including the now-extinct Jennet.

HANDSOME AND REFINED

The Jennet was rather plain, but it had a particularly comfortable and smooth four-beat gait that it passed on to its offspring. Mixing with other breeds produced a handsome, refined creature that had a *paso fino*, or "fine step." When the foals are born and struggle to their feet, they move naturally in this gait.

BEST-KEPT SECRET

It is said that the Paso Fino is the Americas' best-kept secret, but it is rapidly gaining a reputation as the "smoothest riding horse in the world." Its supremely comfortable gait is a lateral pace, with little up-and-down movement in the hindquarters or in the shoulders of the horse, so there is no jarring to the rider. Its "fine step" is unique to the breed.

VERSATILE AND POPULAR

But it is not all about the gait. The Paso Fino is a beautiful animal, full of energy, athletic ability, and stamina, yet kind and gentle to handle. Its versatility means it can adapt to different climates and uses, and it is now found throughout North and South America.

FACT FILE

HEIGHT: up to 15.2hh

COLOR: all colors

CHARACTER: gentle, kind, easy to train

USES: trail riding, showing, ranching, rodeo, Western riding, endurance, dressage

THE PERUVIAN PASO

Although it shares some common ancestry with the Paso Fino, Peru's national horse is an entirely separate breed. The first horses to arrive in Peru came with Francisco Pizarro in 1531. Mounted on these unfamiliar animals on the battlefield, Pizarro and his troops terrified their Inca enemies, who had never seen such creatures.

AFTER THE INCAS

After the fall of the Inca Empire, the conquistadors' horses were still vital for communication, but the Spanish soon found another use for their mounts—on their vast plantations, which were then more common than ranches. The long distances they needed to cover resulted in the development of what is now the Peruvian Paso.

SMALL AND SMOOTH

Long distances needed a horse that had stamina, and long hours spent in the saddle required a comfortable ride. The difficult terrain, with its narrow mountain passes and dense rainforest, required a smaller horse than the taller breeds used on ranches. An athletic, lighter creature with a smooth pace was much better suited to life in Peru.

GUARANTEED GAITS

Just forty or so years ago, the Peruvian Paso was virtually unheard of outside Peru. It remained pure of outside blood for four centuries and its wonderful, smooth gait is guaranteed to be passed on to its offspring. It performs a gait known as the *termino*, in which its forelegs move outward from the shoulder, like the arms of a swimmer.

FACT FILE

HEIGHT: up to 15.2hh

COLORS: all solid colors

CHARACTER: intelligent, spirited, gentle

USES: showing, riding, endurance, dressage

THE MANGALARGA MARCHADOR

Just saying the name of Brazil's national horse makes you want to dance! And that's what these beautiful horses seem to do: the word *marcha* describes their smooth and rhythmic gait. "Mangalarga" comes from the horse farm where many of the early horses were bred. Carefully kept records means that modern Marchadors can be traced back twenty generations or more.

THE MARCHA GAITS

There are three marchas: the marcha picada, which is sometimes described as broken pace, with more lateral movement than diagonal; the marcha batida, which is the opposite; and the marcha de centro, where the lateral and diagonal movements are equal. In all marcha gaits, the horse always has some contact with the ground, so the rider feels secure.

ROYAL BEGINNINGS

When Napoleon's armies threatened Portugal in 1807, the royal family fled to Brazil, taking their best horses with them. These included a stallion called Sublime, who was crossed with Brazil's existing horses, which were mostly of Spanish stock. The resulting animals were initially known as Sublime horses.

FACT FILE

HEIGHT: 16hh

COLOR: mostly gray, bay, dun, and chestnut

CHARACTER: intelligent, docile, kind

USES: endurance, showing, pleasure riding

STRENGTH AND GRACE

The Marchador is an exceptionally good-looking horse, but it is also strong and tough. In 1994, two Brazilian men completed an 8,694-mi. (13,992-km) trail ride to prove the stamina of the breed. For a year and a half they rode all day and rested all night, finishing the journey with the same horses.

A New Life Begins

All baby animals are adorable, but there's something about a newborn foal's wide-eyed gawkiness that captures the heart—whether it represents the next generation of a valuable racing dynasty, or that of a much-loved family pony.

FINDING THEIR FEET

When wild horses roamed freely in forests and grasslands, they were prey animals, not predators. A horse has two basic defense mechanisms—fight or flight—and it mostly relies on the second option. Over many thousands of years, horses have evolved into tall animals that use their long legs to outrun their hunters.

A BABY AT RISK

A newborn foal is especially vulnerable, and so is its mother. Mares tend to give birth at night, or very early in the morning—the quietest time of day. In the wild, a mare will give birth at night because she can hide her foal in the darkness until it is able to run away from predators. Even today, a mare may delay foaling until nighttime, when she feels most safe.

LEARNING TO STAND

When a foal is born, it is weak and unsteady, but after about 30 minutes it will try to stand up. In the wild, this is vital, since it must be able to flee with its mother if danger threatens. It may make several attempts to stand, wobbling unsteadily on its spindly legs before toppling to the ground. But an hour after birth, the foal should be fairly steady on its feet.

SURVIVAL INSTINCTS

Once it is able to stand for more than a few seconds, the foal will take its first, shaky steps. Its first action once it can walk is to seek its mother's udder to suckle, taking in the nutrients it needs for survival. Perhaps two hours after it is born, the foal will be able to trot and gallop.

GROWING UP

For the first month or so the foal will stay close to its mother, but as it gets braver and more confident, it will leave her side to play in the field. If there are other mares and foals, it will interact with them. The youngsters will engage in mock battles, rearing, striking out with their feet, and running away.

LEARNING TO SURVIVE

Although the foal's antics may look innocent and carefree, it is learning all the time. The bucking, kicking, and galloping will strengthen its bones and muscles. As it spins and twists, it learns how to use its body to stay balanced. All this goes toward preparing the foal for its future—but hopefully not to flee the danger that stalked its long-ago ancestors.

Horses
From
Around the World

Arabian influence stretches across the globe, from the mighty Percheron of France, to the pretty Welsh Mountain Pony of the United Kingdom, and the handsome, fleet-footed Orlov Trotter of old Russia. The beauty of the world's horses is glorious in its diversity.

THE LIPIZZANER

Just six stallions founded the modern Lipizzaner—known best for their captivating performances as part of the Spanish Riding School of Vienna. The stallions were Conversano, a black horse of Arabian origin; Favory, a dun; Maestoso, a white horse of Spanish descent; Neapolitano, a bay; Pluto, who had Danish blood; and the gray Siglavy, an Arabian.

SPANISH AND ARABIAN

The Lipizzaner is renowned for its beauty, strength, and nobility—all of which owe as much to its Spanish heritage as to the Arabian. White horses have always been highly prized—they pulled the chariots of kings and emperors and, since Roman times, have represented peace and justice.

ROYAL BACKGROUND

The breed was founded by Archduke Charles II, brother of the Holy Roman Emporer Maximilian I, at the court stud farm of Lipizza, near Trieste in Italy, in 1580. The stud farm still exists today, in what is now Lipica, in Slovenia. The stud farm's "dancing white horses" were showcased in the Spanish Riding School, performing haute ecole, or "high school," movements and "airs above the ground."

FACT FILE

HEIGHT: 16hh

COLOR: born black or brown, they almost always turn gray, but the Spanish Riding School always keeps a dark Lipizzaner for luck

CHARACTER: fiery, intelligent, trainable

USES: showing, driving, riding, dressage

THE UNITED STATES TO THE RESCUE

During outbreaks of war, the Lipizzaners were moved to safety, but in 1943, during World War II, the breed was almost lost. The German High Command seized mares and foals from Austria, Italy, and Yugoslavia, and held them at Hostau, in what was Czechoslovakia. General George Patton gave the United States Army's protection to the stallions and ordered the Second Cavalry to retrieve the mares from Czechoslovakia.

THE FRIESIAN

Its beauty will take your breath away, but the handsome black Friesian was developed as a warhorse in the northwest of Europe, in what is now the Netherlands. Ancient writings mention that horses like these were used in battle by Friesian troops in Roman Britain, and what would become the modern Friesian breed dates from at least the 1200s.

REFINED AND PROUD

During the Crusades, the Friesian was undoubtedly influenced by Arabian and Spanish blood. This is evident in its refined head and proud bearing, as well as its high-stepping knee action. However, it has not been influenced by the Thoroughbred and, during the past two centuries, it has been kept pure.

HEAVY ARMOR

Knights of old wore heavy armor into battle, so their warhorses had to be extremely strong to carry them, but still be able to maneuver. The Friesian more than ticked these boxes and, during the 15th and 16th centuries, its suppleness and agility made it popular in riding schools in France and Spain. In the late 1600s, it was taken to America by the Dutch in the settlement called New Amsterdam, which later became New York.

ELEGANT AND ATHLETIC

The coal-black Friesian was much in demand as a carriage horse and is still seen today pulling hearses at funerals, proudly bearing plumes on its head. But its athletic ability also makes it suitable for equestrian sports, including dressage and Western riding. They are not bred for jumping, but are still able to clear small obstacles.

FACT FILE

HEIGHT: up to 15.3hh

COLOR: always black (a small white star is the only permitted white marking)

CHARACTER: strong, gentle, kind

USES: carriage driving, riding, showing, dressage, Western

THE HANOVERIAN

This breed is undoubtedly one of the horse world's most impressive success stories. The Hanoverian is what is known as a "warmblood"—the result of crossing a heavy draft horse with a Thoroughbred. The Hanoverian takes its name from its birthplace in the northern German state of Lower Saxony, the former kingdom of Hanover, which has been breeding horses for 300 years.

GOING INTO BATTLE

The State Stud of Lower Saxony was established at Celle in 1735. The stud farm's early goal was to produce good-looking, good-moving, and athletic horses to pull carriages. Later, these handsome creatures were required by the cavalry and artillery, so they still needed considerable strength and agility.

HANDSOME IS...

It wasn't until after World War II that the Hanoverian horse really came into its own as a riding and competition horse. It was used for recreational riding, as well as necessary work on the farm, and still had to have good looks and a good gait for pulling carriages. The Hanoverian possessed all these qualities, but also proved itself a supreme competition horse, excelling at eventing, show jumping, and dressage.

FAMOUS HANOVERIANS

The names of famous modern Hanoverian horses can be found etched on trophies in all Olympic disciplines. Top show jumper Scott Brash rides one called Hello Annie with great success. The dressage sensation Woodlander Farouche is Hanoverian, and so is Ingrid Klimke's double Olympic three-day eventing team gold medalist, FRH Butts Abraxxas.

FACT FILE

HEIGHT: 17hh

COLOR: brown, chestnut, bay, black, gray

CHARACTER: intelligent, even-tempered, rideable

USES: competition, driving

THE TRAKEHNER

In the early 18th century, King Frederick Wilhelm I of Prussia, in northern Germany, wanted his soldiers to have a warhorse that was faster, sounder, and more enduring than those of his enemies. He established a stud farm at Trakehnen in East Prussia, where he crossed the small native mares, called *schwaike*, to Thoroughbreds and Arabians.

THE BEST RESULTS

Various other bloodlines were used in developing the original Trakehner, but King Frederick Wilhelm found that he got the best results—handsome, friendly equines that possessed great athletic ability—with the Thoroughbreds and Arabians, so he used those crosses. He kept the best stock for breeding, and sold the rest as "riding horses."

ELEGANT WARMBLOOD

Of all the warmblood breeds, the Trakehner has the most Thoroughbred blood, which can clearly be seen in its handsome appearance. It is more refined than some of the other warmbloods, with an elegant head, long, graceful neck, and deep, sloping shoulder that allows it to move so freely. It is renowned for its elastic paces and "floating" trot. It is said that the Trakehner is the competition horse everyone is looking for.

A BREED ALMOST LOST

In 1945, at the end of World War II, East Prussians were forced to flee by the advancing Soviet Army. They packed their belongings into wagons, harnessed their Trakehner horses, and escaped across the frozen bay of the Baltic Sea, between Prussia and the West. Many did not make it, as the ice cracked under their feet. Fewer than 10 percent of the horses in East Prussia reached the safety of West Germany.

FACT FILE

HEIGHT: 17hh

COLOR: most colors

CHARACTER: friendly, athletic, trainable

USES: all Olympic disciplines

THE SELLE FRANÇAIS

It may be one of the youngest warmblood breeds, but the Selle Français has already made its mark as a supreme competition horse. The Olympic show jumping champion Nino De Buissonnets is a prime example. It wasn't until the 20th century that horses were bred in France specifically for sports rather than for war.

THE PROTOTYPE

The breed originated in Normandy, when breeders imported Thoroughbreds and trotters from England to cross with native stock. Two types emerged: a speedy harness horse known as the French Trotter, and the Anglo-Norman. The Anglo-Norman is recognized as the prototype for the Selle Français.

A LOCAL MIX

Various different local breeds have had some influence on the Selle Français, including Vendéen, Charollais, Limousin, and Charentais. After World War II the French put the emphasis on breeding a horse for riding, and that is how the Cheval de Selle Français, or "French saddle horse," came about.

FACT FILE

HEIGHT: up to 17hh

COLOR: chestnut is most common

CHARACTER: clever, brave, calm

USES: all Olympic disciplines, racing

MODEL GOOD LOOKS

Thanks to the use of Thoroughbred and Anglo-Arab blood, the modern Selle Français, like all warmbloods, is extremely handsome. But those good looks are combined with strength, speed, and intelligence. It has a neat, attractive head set on a long neck, a nicely sloping shoulder, deep chest, and long, muscular body.

73

THE HAFLINGER

A tiny village in the Southern Tyrolean Mountains of what is now Austria and northern Italy gave its name to this enchanting breed. Many of the farms and villages in the area were reachable only by narrow paths and steep mountain trails, which called for an agile and sure-footed horse.

THE FIRST STALLION

The Haflinger—named for the village of Hafling—is Middle Eastern in origin, with the foundation stallion being 249 Folie, who was foaled in 1874. He was by an Arabian stallion out of a native Tyrolean mare. All modern Haflingers can be traced back to Folie through seven different stallion lines: A, B, M, N, S, ST, and W, although only the A-line and the W-line trace directly to him.

PERFECT FOR PACK

There is no carthorse blood in the Haflinger. Carthorses, which were generally of sturdy build, would not have been much use in the Tyrol. The compact little Haflinger was ideally suited to working on the high mountain farms, and in the steep fields and forests. They were excellent pack animals, used to transport food between farms and villages, and are still used today for pack or lumber work.

FACT FILE

HEIGHT: up to 14.3hh

COLOR: shades of chestnut, from pale gold to liver

CHARACTER: friendly, eager, willing

USES: all riding, driving, pack

CHARMING HORSE

In addition to its glorious color, the Haflinger is a charming creature, with an endearing, people-loving nature. It is willing to work, which makes it very child-friendly, and can turn its hoof to almost any equestrian discipline. From the mountains of the Tyrol, the Haflinger has spread to 60 countries, and there are a quarter of a million registered.

THE PERCHERON

Of all the heavy horse breeds, the Percheron must be the most elegant, a trait that comes from its Arabian heritage. It was originally bred at Le Perche, in Normandy, France, and was probably introduced to England by William the Conqueror in 1066. But its origins are thought to be much older—dating back to the 8th century.

FROM WARHORSE TO FARM HORSE

The early horses carried knights wearing heavy armor into battle. But a lighter horse was later required for working the land. The founding stallion was named Jean Le Blanc, the offspring of a local draft mare and an Arabian sire called Gallipoly, foaled in 1823. The Arabian blood gave the breed its high-stepping action and refined good looks.

AMERICAN STUDBOOK

The first Percherons were imported to the United Sates in 1839 by Edward Harris of Moorestown, New Jersey. He made two attempts to bring in eight horses, but only two survived the journey—a mare called Joan and a stallion named Diligence. The stallion lived up to his name, siring more than 400 offspring. The first American Percheron studbook was opened in 1876.

THE ARAB INFLUENCE

The high proportion of Arabian blood in this heavy horse breed is evident in its fine head and in its color—it is always gray or black. It has the wide forehead, wide nostrils, and long neck seen in the Arab. Its legs have less hair than other draft breeds, with a powerful forearm and muscular thighs. Its lively action and high-set tail also tell of its exotic breeding.

FACT FILE

HEIGHT: up to 18hh

COLOR: gray or black

CHARACTER: kind, intelligent, placid

USES: riding, driving, showing

THE FJORD

Four thousand years ago, the horses that had migrated to Norway, on the Scandinavian peninsula, were first domesticated by humans. Remains found at Viking burial sites indicate that the Fjord has been selectively bred for 2,000 years. Today, this strong and resilient little horse is one of Norway's national symbols.

PRIMITIVE MARKINGS

The Fjord is an attractive animal, nearly always dun in color, and often showing the "primitive" markings of striped legs, black points, and a black dorsal stripe down its back. Because of these "wild" markings, it is likely that the Fjord is related to the Asiatic Wild Horse.

UNIQUE MANE

A unique characteristic of the Fjord is its striking mane. The center hair is black, while the outer hair is white. The mane is cut short so that it will stand erect and is cut into a crescent shape to emphasize the graceful curve of the horse's neck. The white outer hair is then trimmed slightly shorter than the dark inner hair to display the dramatic dark stripe.

HIGH REGARD

The Norwegians are so proud of their native breed that the following flowery description was written: "The eyes should be like the mountain lakes on a midsummer evening, big and bright. A bold bearing of the neck, like a lad from the mountains on his way to his beloved. The temperament as lively as a waterfall in spring, and still good-natured."

FACT FILE

HEIGHT: around 14.2hh

COLOR: all shades of dun

CHARACTER: biddable, intelligent, kind

USES: riding, trekking, driving, pack

THE WELSH

Arabian influence is clear to see in the pretty head of the Welsh Mountain Pony. Its wide forehead, large eyes, and dished profile give it an Arab-type appearance. This probably dates back to Roman times, when the invading armies brought horses that had been captured during their African campaigns. They left them behind when they withdrew in 410 A.D.

EVADING THE KING'S DEMAND

King Henry VIII ordered that all equines under the height of 15hh should be destroyed, but the Welsh Mountain Ponies, hiding on rugged hillsides in desolate spaces, evaded capture. The ponies that survived were the toughest and hardiest of all, and those that exist today still run on the Welsh hills, in bands of mares led by a stallion.

A WORKING BREED

Despite its undeniable beauty, the Welsh Mountain Pony is far from being simply a "pretty toy." It would have pulled chariots in the distant past, and since then it has worked deep underground in coal mines, on ranches, and on farms, serving both the poor and high society. The bigger Welsh Section C and Section D make excellent riding and driving ponies as well as handsome show animals.

FACT FILE

HEIGHT: up to 12.2hh (Sec A)

COLOR: all solid colors

CHARACTER: spirited, intelligent, gentle

USES: riding, driving, showing

THE STUDBOOK

The Welsh Mountain Pony is known as the Welsh Section A, because the Welsh studbook is divided into four sections. The Section B is a finer pony, more of a riding type. Section C is heavier and larger, standing up to 13.2hh, while the Section D, or Welsh Cob, is a fiery creature that resembles a scaled-up version of the Mountain Pony, but with no upper height limit.

THE SHETLAND

Tiny ponies have lived on the Shetlands—the northernmost islands of the United Kingdom—for 2,000 years, if not more. Their origins probably lie in the ancient tundra ponies that walked across the ice fields and land masses during the last Ice Age, thousands of years ago.

EASTERN INFLUENCE

The Celtic people, who came to Great Britain over the period from about 500 B.C. to 100 B.C., brought with them other equines, probably with Eastern blood. They bred these to the native animals and the result was a small, strong, and hardy pony that worked alongside its island owners.

SEAWEED FOR FOOD

Because of the isolated location of the Shetland Isles, there were few imported horses, so the pony remained pure for centuries. No place in Shetland is farther than 4 mi. (6 km) from the sea, and it is part of the local legend that, during the worst winters, lack of grazing would drive some ponies to forage for seaweed along the shoreline.

HIGHLY PRIZED

The ponies worked the land, carried peat and seaweed, and survived on meager rations. Fishermen would even use hairs from their tails as fishing line. For all these things, the Shetland was highly prized. One of the earliest laws recorded in Shetland cautioned would-be thieves not to "cut any other man's horse-tail or mane under the pain [of a fine] of ten pounds"—a huge sum of money in those days.

FACT FILE

HEIGHT: up to 42 in. (107 cm)

COLOR: all colors

CHARACTER: stubborn, intelligent, spirited

USES: riding, pack, driving

THE CONNEMARA

Ireland's west coast is wild, rocky, and lashed by the Atlantic Ocean. Any pony that lived there had to be hardy and sure-footed: one slip could mean certain death. Connemara ponies have lived there for centuries, scraping an existence from desolate moors, bogs, and barren coastline. This hardy pony is now considered Ireland's only native breed.

THE LEGEND

Celtic warriors brought their dun-colored ponies to the island around 2,500 years ago. Some must have broken free, and a wild pony population soon roamed the ancient mountains. Legend says that when the Spanish Armada sank off the Connemara coast in the 16th century, some of the Spanish horses swam to shore and mated with the native stock.

FACT FILE

HEIGHT: up to 14.2hh

COLOR: all solid colors

CHARACTER: gentle, intelligent, sound

USES: all riding, hunting, jumping, showing

A HARD LIFE

If existence was tough for Connemara's ponies, it was doubly so for the region's farmers. They had large families to feed and money was scarce. For some, to get a decent pony, the only option was to capture one from the mountain and tame it. Preferably they would catch a mare who could give them a foal to sell.

IN DEMAND

Those early equines no doubt worked hard. But today the Connemara pony is much in demand. It is good-looking and gentle, but retains the athleticism that allowed it to live on the mountains. It makes a wonderful child's pony and is popular in the show ring. Whatever its heritage, the Connemara is here to stay.

THE SUFFOLK

Britain's oldest heavy horse breed is the Suffolk. All modern Suffolks can trace their origins back to one stallion, called Crisp's Horse of Ufford. Foaled in 1768, he is considered the breed's foundation sire, but he was not actually the first Suffolk. These animals were first bred as huge, heavy warhorses, but the breed was shaped by the land it worked and lived on in Norfolk and Suffolk in the east of England.

WORKING THE LAND

The Suffolk's birthplace is bordered on the north, east, and south by the North Sea, and on the west by the fens—low-lying, flat marshland that was drained for farming. The farmers of this region needed a strong horse to plow the heavy clay soil. It had to be tough, sound, docile, and long-living. Those fenland farmers made their living from what they could grow, not the horses they bred, so the Suffolk remained fairly pure.

SHORT AND STOCKY

The Suffolk is smaller than other draft breeds and, unlike the Shire, has no "feather"—long, silky hair—on its lower legs. This would not be helpful in the sticky red clay of its home counties. The Suffolk was initially unaffected by the coming of motorized tractors, because few of the early machines could cope with the local clay soil.

A LEG AT EACH CORNER

The Suffolk is a handsome creature. It has a square, solid appearance, braced on short, sturdy legs. This "leg-at-each-corner" stance gave the breed its charming nickname of "Suffolk Punch." It is always chestnut, ranging from bright golden to dark liver, with a comparatively small, intelligent head, arching neck, and a short, strong back.

FACT FILE

HEIGHT: 16.3hh

COLOR: always chestnut

CHARACTER: calm, gentle, docile

USES: showing, driving, agriculture

THE SHIRE

England's most famous heavy draft breed takes its name from the Saxon word *schyran*, meaning "to shear, or divide." Its English form, shire, appears on the end of many British county names. The draft horse was descended from heavy warhorses and was first called a Shire by Henry VIII in the early 16th century. It had previously been known as the Great Horse, the Cart-Horse, the English Black, and the Lincolnshire Giant.

INDUSTRIAL REVOLUTION

As roads improved during the 18th century, the Shire became much in demand for draft work, as well as pulling plows on farms, where it had replaced oxen. During the Industrial Revolution, a nationwide network of canals was built, so horses were needed to walk along the banks, pulling the barges.

FACT FILE

HEIGHT: 17.3hh and over

COLOR: bay, black, gray, chestnut

CHARACTER: calm, gentle, biddable

USES: driving, showing, riding, ceremonial

A BLEAK OUTLOOK

Later on, the Industrial Revolution almost proved to be the Shire's downfall. As trains replaced barges, and tractors replaced plows, the mighty draft horses fell out of favor. Numbers dropped from more than a million to just a few thousand in the 1960s. Even in the United States, where the breed had first been imported in the 1880s, it failed to retain its early popularity. In the early 1900s, there were around 6,700 Shires in North America. By 1959, there were only 25.

SHIRE SUCCESS STORY

In England, a small group of dedicated breeders managed to save valuable bloodlines and keep the breed going. Today, the Shire Horse Society is in good shape and holds an annual show every March. It is well attended and Shire enthusiasts visit from the world over to celebrate the beauty and heart of the mighty Shire. The world record height is over 20hh.

THE ORLOV TROTTER

After the Russian emperor Peter III was assassinated in 1762, his wife took the throne as Catherine the Great. As thanks for his role in this coup, Count Alexei Orlov was given a huge tract of land in the steppe region of central Russia. It was here that Count Orlov founded the Khrenovsky Stud, where the Orlov breed was later developed. The farm is still in operation today, and some of the superb stone structures built by the count are still being used.

THE BEAUTIFUL BREED

The Orlov Trotter was bred to be a harness horse of considerable speed and great beauty. The Count's wealth, popularity, and political connections enabled him to acquire the very best horses from Arabia, Persia, Turkey, Poland, Holland, Spain, and Germany. Among these was an Arabian stallion called Smetanka, who was silver-gray and long-backed. An autopsy after the horse's death revealed that he had 19 ribs, instead of the usual 18.

STAMINA AND SPEED

After some experiments, the Count bred Smetanka to a dun-colored Danish mare, producing a gray stallion called Polkan I in 1778. Smetanka died in 1779, so the Count bred his son, Polkan, to Friesian mares, including an unusual gray. The resulting son, a gray called Bars I, foaled in 1784, is regarded as the foundation sire for the breed. As well as their ground-covering but smooth trot, the Orlov horses had great stamina and glorious beauty.

TROIKA AND THE OLYMPICS

Traditionally, the Orlov was a handsome carriage horse, but it was also in demand for the troika, a sled-type vehicle pulled by three horses. The center horse trots, while the two outside horses gallop. In modern times, the Orlov has shown its skill in sporting events: at the Olympic Games in both 2004 and 2008, the Russian rider Alexandra Korelova competed an Orlov Trotter called Balagur, a former police horse, in the dressage arena.

FACT FILE

HEIGHT: 17hh

COLOR: mostly gray

CHARACTER: sound, quiet, intelligent

USES: harness, riding, showing

THE MARWARI

This beautiful horse comes from a time of castles and heroes, intrigue and passion, dark deeds and mythological horses. The elegant Marwari captures the essence of a period when "the ocean was churned to extract nectar for the gods … a period when horses had wings." This may not be completely true, but the Marwari was held in high regard in its native India, where it had been known since at least the 12th century.

BANISHED TO THE DESERT

The Rathore warrior clan of the Rajput people were driven from their kingdom to a region known as Maru Pradesh, meaning "land of death." They were proud of their tough but beautiful equines and once fielded a cavalry of more than 50,000 horses. There were said to be only three ways a Marwari would leave a battlefield: alive and victorious; carrying its wounded master to safety; or being devoured by vultures after laying down its life for its master.

HOMING INSTINCT

As well as its speed and beauty, the Marwari is renowned for its homing instinct. It saved the lives of countless riders, bringing them back when they got lost in the desert. Its tiny, extravagantly curled ears had supremely good hearing, too, so it could catch the sounds of possible danger from much farther away than any human, giving horse and rider an early warning.

THE MARWARI TODAY

As the role of the horse in battle declined, so did the numbers of Marwaris and, during the days of British rule, the breed was almost lost. However, the Maharaja Gaj Singh II wanted to preserve India's national horse and, under his patronage, the All India Marwari Horse Society was founded in 1998. Today the Marwari is particularly popular as a safari horse, because of its loyalty, gentleness, and smooth, comfortable gait.

THE CASPIAN

In 1965, an American named Louise Firouz discovered herds of small horses living in the Mazanderan province of northern Iran. These narrow little creatures were horses, not ponies, although they stood less than 12hh, and were thought to have been extinct for 1,000 years. They are believed by some to be the forerunner to the Arabian, the foundation of so many of the world's modern breeds. Firouz named them Caspian horses.

HORSES OF KINGS

Ancient artifacts and writings show that the ancient kings of this region favored small, elegant horses. King Darius the Great, who ruled from 522 B.C. to 486 B.C., valued them so highly that they pulled his chariot in lion hunts. His palace at Persepolis (near modern Tehran) shows a frieze of animals on its main staircase, featuring small horses that reach only to their leaders' waists. In those days, they were known as Lydean horses, but they were undoubtedly the first Caspians.

A LIVING LINK

More recently, small, delicate equines were seen along the southern shores of the Caspian Sea, as well as in the mountains and villages around it. They were known locally as Mouleki or Pouseki ponies and were used for pack or pulling carts. Slender leg bones found in an ancient site in northern Iran were originally thought to have been from a wild ass, but when they were compared with those of the Pouseki, they were found to be very similar.

GIFT HORSES

Firouz wanted the little horses to be part of her riding school just outside Tehran, and she established a herd of Caspians. Of these, seven mares and six stallions became the foundation stock for a breeding center she founded at Norouzebad, near Tehran. In 1971, a mare and a stallion were presented to the husband of Queen Elizabeth II of the United Kingdom. A respected horseman in his own right, he recommended that more Caspians were exported to the UK, Australia, and New Zealand, and the ancient breed was saved.

FACT FILE

HEIGHT: 11.2hh

COLOR: bay, black, gray, chestnut

CHARACTER: biddable, intelligent, gentle

USES: riding, harness, showing, pack

INDEX